101
Kitchen Secrets

FAMILIUS

PUBLISHED BY FAMILIUS LLC, WWW.FAMILIUS.COM
PO BOX 1130, SANGER, CA 93657

FAMILIUS BOOKS ARE AVAILABLE AT SPECIAL DISCOUNTS FOR BULK PURCHASES,
WHETHER FOR SALES PROMOTIONS OR FOR FAMILY OR CORPORATE USE. FOR MORE
INFORMATION, CONTACT FAMILIUS SALES AT ORDERS@FAMILIUS.COM.

LIBRARY OF CONGRESS CONTROL NUMBER: 2024940976

PRINT ISBN 9781641708739
EBOOK ISBN 9798889360372

PRINTED IN CHINA

EDITED BY PEG SANDKAM
COVER AND BOOK DESIGN BY BROOKE JORDEN
ILLUSTRATIONS LICENSED FROM VECTEEZY

10 9 8 7 6 5 4 3 2 1

FIRST EDITION

101

Kitchen Secrets

CUT DOWN ON DISHES, COST & TIME IN THE KITCHEN

JASON GOLDSTEIN
@CHOPHAPPY

FOR SECRETS TO:

SAVE DISHES . . . . #1

SAVE MONEY . . . . #33

SAVE TIME . . . . #67

HI! I'M JASON GOLDSTEIN. YOU MIGHT KNOW ME BY MY SOCIAL MEDIA HANDLE, @CHOPHAPPY.

I'M HERE TO DISH ALL THE BEST SECRETS THAT WILL MAKE YOUR LIFE EASIER IN THE KITCHEN!

WITH THESE HACKS, YOU'LL USE FEWER DISHES, CUT DOWN ON WASTE AND OVERSPENDING, AND SPEND LESS TIME COOKING SO YOU CAN SPEND MORE TIME EATING. JUST KIDDING! KIND OF . . .

WITH THESE 101 KITCHEN SECRETS, YOU'LL BE COOKING LIKE A PRO IN NO TIME!

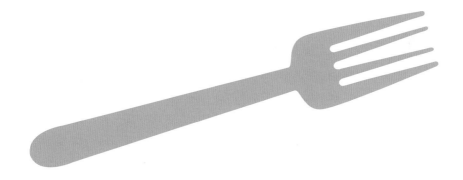

SAVE DISHES

MAKE CLEANUP A BREEZE WITH THESE EASY TIPS

SAVE MONEY

SAVE TIME

Secret #1

VIRAL BREADING STATION HACK.

USE A SHEET PAN AND CREATE THREE SECTIONS WITH TINFOIL: ONE SECTION FOR FLOUR, ONE SECTION FOR EGGS, AND ONE SECTION FOR BREAD CRUMBS. WHEN DONE, ROLL UP THE TINFOIL AND THROW IT ALL OUT. NO MESS IN THE KITCHEN AND EASY CLEANUP!

Secret #2

LESS MESS WHEN SEARING SHORT RIBS.

INSTEAD OF SEARING YOUR SHORT RIBS OR YOUR BRISKET IN A PAN WITH OIL (WHEN YOUR RECIPE ASKS YOU TO), YOU CAN JUST PUT IT ON A SHEET PAN AND ROAST IT AT 450 DEGREES FOR 15 MINUTES. YOU GET PERFECTLY SEARED BEEF WITHOUT THE MESS! THEN CONTINUE COOKING BASED ON THE RECIPE YOU ARE USING.

Secret # 3

COOK COUSCOUS IN THE SAME BOWL YOU ARE SERVING IT IN.

POUR 1 CUP COUSCOUS AND 1 CUP HOT LIQUID (WATER, CHICKEN BROTH, OR VEGGIE BROTH HEATED IN THE MICROWAVE FOR 2 MINUTES) IN A BOWL AND MIX. COVER FOR 10 MINUTES THEN ADD YOUR FAVORITE COOKED PROTEIN AND VEGGIES AND SERVE. NO NEED TO USE EXTRA POTS OR PANS.

Secret #4

SLOW COOKER SPAGHETTI AND MEATBALLS.

INSTEAD OF USING SEPARATE DISHES TO BOIL THE PASTA, HEAT THE SAUCE, COOK THE MEATBALLS, AND SERVE THE FOOD, TRY THIS HACK. PUT 1 POUND UNCOOKED SPAGHETTI, 1 JAR OF YOUR FAVORITE MARINARA SAUCE, 2 CUPS WATER, AND MEATBALLS INTO A SLOW COOKER. COOK FOR 5 HOURS ON LOW. BRING THE SLOW COOKER TO THE TABLE AND SERVE THE FINISHED SPAGHETTI OUT OF IT.

Secret #5

SHEET PAN MEATBALLS RECIPE.

PLACE UNCOOKED MEATBALLS ON A SHEET PAN. BAKE FOR 20 MINUTES AT 425 DEGREES. THEN ADD THE MARINARA SAUCE DIRECTLY ON THE MEATBALLS AND HEAT IT UP WITH THE MEATBALLS FOR 10 MINUTES.

MAC AND CHEESE ALL IN A MUG.

MIX 1/2 CUP UNCOOKED MACARONI PASTA, 1/2 CUP WATER, 3 SLICES OF YOUR FAVORITE CHEESE, 2 TABLESPOONS PLAIN GREEK YOGURT, AND YOUR FAVORITE SEASONINGS IN A MUG. MICROWAVE FOR 4 MINUTES AND STIR, THEN PLACE ANOTHER SLICE OF CHEESE ON TOP AND COOK FOR 1 MORE MINUTE.

Secret #7

COOK YOUR BACON ON A SHEET PAN SO THERE IS NO SPLATTER!

SPREAD OUT THE BACON ON A SHEET PAN LINED WITH TINFOIL. BAKE AT 400 DEGREES FOR 10 MINUTES AND HAVE PERFECTLY CRISP BACON WITHOUT SPLATTERING OIL ALL OVER THE COUNTER. JUST ROLL UP THE TINFOIL AND THROW IT AWAY. NO NEED TO CLEAN UP THE SHEET PAN EITHER!

Secret #8

MASON JAR GARLIC PEELER.

TO PEEL A WHOLE BULB OF GARLIC WITHOUT A MESS, PUT THE BULB IN A MASON JAR AND SEAL. SHAKE THE MASON JAR FOR 1-2 MINUTES AND THE CLOVES WILL SEPARATE WITH EASE.

Secret #9

NO LEMON SEEDS!

INSTEAD OF USING A STRAINER TO CATCH SEEDS WHEN YOU SQUEEZE LEMON JUICE, JUST SQUEEZE THE LEMON CUT-SIDE UP AND THE SEEDS WILL STAY IN THE LEMON— NO EXTRA KITCHEN TOOLS NEEDED!

COOK SCALLOPS IN OVEN WITH LESS SPLATTER.

WANT TO AVOID THE MESS OF SEARING SCALLOPS IN A PAN? PLACE VEGGIES OR BEANS ON THE BOTTOM OF A CASSEROLE DISH AND MIX IN 2 TABLESPOONS EACH OF OLIVE OIL AND YOUR FAVORITE SEASONINGS. TOP WITH 1 1/2 POUNDS SCALLOPS SEASONED WITH 2 TEASPOONS EACH OF SALT AND PEPPER. BAKE ON THE MIDDLE RACK FOR 15 MINUTES AT 400 DEGREES AND TOP WITH PESTO. THIS MAKES AN ALL-IN-ONE DISH AND AVOIDS THE SPLATTERING THAT COMES FROM THE TRADITIONAL WAY OF COOKING SCALLOPS.

Secret #11

CASSEROLE SAUSAGE AND PEPPERS.

NO NEED TO MAKE A MESS IN THE KITCHEN BY FRYING UP SAUSAGE. ADD YOUR SAUSAGE, PEPPERS, AND ANY OTHER INGREDIENTS FOR YOUR RECIPE PLUS 1 JAR OF YOUR FAVORITE MARINARA SAUCE TO A CASSEROLE DISH. BAKE FOR 20 MINUTES AT 400 DEGREES AND EVERYTHING IS DONE IN ONE DISH.

Secret # **12**

USE BOTH SIDES OF THE CUTTING BOARD.

PREP YOUR VEGGIES FIRST THEN FLIP THE CUTTING BOARD AND PREP YOUR PROTEIN. THIS WAY YOU AVOID CROSS CONTAMINATION BUT YOU DON'T NEED TO CLEAN TWO CUTTING BOARDS.

Secret #13

PLASTIC WRAP YOUR ROLLING PIN.

WRAP YOUR ROLLING PIN IN PLASTIC WRAP BEFORE YOU ROLL OUT DOUGH SO YOU DON'T HAVE TO WASH THE ROLLING PIN. WHEN YOU'RE FINISHED, JUST THROW OUT THE PLASTIC WRAP.

LINT ROLL THE MESS IN THE KITCHEN.

IF YOU HAVE LOTS OF CRUMBS ON THE COUNTER WHEN COOKING, USE A LINT ROLLER! THE CRUMBS WILL STICK RIGHT TO THE PAPER.

Secret #15

POMEGRANATE HACK.

AVOID THE RED-STAINED HANDS AND COUNTER FROM
PREPARING POMEGRANATE ON A CUTTING BOARD. FIRST,
FILL A BOWL WITH WATER. THEN CUT THE POMEGRANATE
IN HALF AND SQUEEZE THE HALVES UNDERWATER TO
DISLODGE AND SEPARATE THE SEEDS WITHOUT A MESS.

Secret #16

SPRAY YOUR CHEESE GRATER WITH COOKING SPRAY.

SPRAY COOKING SPRAY ON YOUR CHEESE GRATER AND THE CHEESE WON'T GET STUCK IN THE CREVICES, WHICH MAKES THE GRATER MUCH EASIER TO CLEAN.

Secret #17

SELF-CONTAINED MASHED BANANAS.

INSTEAD OF USING A MASHER OR A FORK, JUST MASH
BANANAS WITHIN THE PEEL.

Secret #18

PAPER TOWEL HACK FOR DRAINING GREASE.

TO DRAIN FAT WHEN COOKING GROUND BEEF, USE TONGS TO HOLD A PAPER TOWEL OVER THE PAN. TILT THE PAN, AND THE PAPER TOWEL WILL ABSORB THE LIQUID.

Secret #19

TRY AN ONION SCRUB FOR YOUR CAST-IRON SKILLET.

TO EASILY REMOVE RUST OR FOOD STUCK ON YOUR CAST-IRON SKILLET, CUT AN ONION IN HALF, HEAT UP THE CAST-IRON, AND RUB THE CUT SIDE OF THE ONION ON THE PAN. ALL THE GUNK WILL STICK TO THE ONION AND MAKE CLEANUP EASY AND FAST!

PLASTIC WRAP HACK.

YOU CAN WRAP YOUR FOOD MORE EFFICIENTLY BY
STORING YOUR PLASTIC WRAP IN THE REFRIGERATOR.
THE COLD AIR KEEPS THE PLASTIC WRAP FROM STICKING
TO ITSELF, WHICH MAKES IT EASIER TO WRAP FOODS
WITHOUT GETTING THE PLASTIC WRAP ALL TANGLED UP.
YOU'LL USE LESS PLASTIC WRAP AND WILL NOT NEED TO
STORE YOUR LEFTOVERS IN A DIFFERENT CONTAINER.

Secret #21

EASY QUESO IN A CASSEROLE DISH.

INSTEAD OF MESSING UP A POT BY MELTING CHEESE, YOU CAN MAKE QUESO IN A CASSEROLE DISH. MIX 3 POUNDS GRATED CHEDDAR CHEESE, 1 TABLESPOON CORNSTARCH, 1 CAN OF EVAPORATED MILK, 1 CUP SALSA, 3 SCALLIONS (CHOPPED), AND THE JUICE OF 1 LIME IN A CASSEROLE DISH. BAKE AT 400 DEGREES FOR 10 MINUTES. SERVE IN THE SAME CASSEROLE DISH WITH CHIPS AND ENJOY!

WINE BOTTLE RAVIOLI CUTTER.

MAKING HOMEMADE RAVIOLI? DON'T DIRTY A PASTA
CUTTER. YOU CAN PRESS OUT RAVIOLI SHAPES WITH THE
BOTTOM OF A WINE BOTTLE.

Secret # 23

MINCED GARLIC WITHOUT THE MESS.

MINCE GARLIC WITHOUT GETTING IT ALL OVER THE KITCHEN. PLACE CLOVES IN A ZIPLOCK BAG AND USE A MEAT TENDERIZER TO SMASH THEM.

USE CONDIMENT BOTTLES FOR NO-MESS PANCAKES.

SAVE YOUR KETCHUP AND MAYO SQUEEZE BOTTLES. YOU CAN POUR PANCAKE BATTER IN THEM AND SQUEEZE IT INTO THE PAN SO YOU DON'T GET BATTER ALL OVER THE KITCHEN.

Secret # 25

NO MORE MESSY MEAT HANDS!

ADD OIL TO YOUR HANDS BEFORE YOU WORK WITH
GROUND BEEF TO AVOID THE BEEF STICKING TO YOU!

Secret #26

SHUCK CORN WITH EASE AND NO MESS.

CUT 1 INCH OFF THE END OF THE COB. PUT THE ENTIRE COB, INCLUDING THE HUSK, INTO THE MICROWAVE FOR 2 MINUTES. LET THE COB COOL FOR 1 MINUTE. NEXT, HOLD THE UNCUT SIDE WITH A TOWEL AND SQUEEZE THE CORN OUT THROUGH THE CUT END. THE SILK AND HUSK SHOULD COME OFF WITH EASE AND WITHOUT A MESS.

Secret #27

HACK TO MAKE PARCHMENT PAPER LAY FLAT.

CRUMBLE UP YOUR PARCHMENT PAPER BEFORE PUTTING IT DOWN ON THE SHEET PAN. THE PARCHMENT WILL NOT MOVE OR ROLL UP AND YOUR FOOD WON'T GET ON THE SHEET PAN.

Secret #28

DON'T THROW AWAY THE BUTTER WRAPPER.

IF YOU ARE MELTING BUTTER IN THE MICROWAVE, PUT THE WAX BUTTER WRAPPER ON TOP OF THE DISH YOU ARE MELTING THE BUTTER IN. THE WRAPPER IS MICROWAVE SAFE AND WILL PREVENT THE BUTTER FROM SPLATTERING ALL OVER YOUR MICROWAVE.

Secret # 29

MUFFIN TIN INGREDIENT PREP

FOR LESS MESS AND FEWER DISHES WHEN PREPARING YOUR INGREDIENTS, GRAB A MUFFIN TIN AND PUT MUFFIN LINERS IN EACH SECTION. AS YOU CHOP EACH INGREDIENT, ADD IT TO A SECTION OF THE MUFFIN TIN. BRING THE MUFFIN TIN TO THE STOVE AND ADD THE INGREDIENTS AS YOU COOK. YOU'LL HAVE FEWER DISHES TO CLEAN, BE MORE ORGANIZED, AND CREATE LESS OF A MESS IN THE KITCHEN.

Secret # 30

SPRAY YOUR MEASURING CUPS.

COAT MEASURING SPOONS AND CUPS WITH COOKING
SPRAY TO AVOID FOOD STICKING TO THEM.

Secret # 31

ROLL OUT DOUGH ON PARCHMENT PAPER.

WHEN BAKING, LAY DOWN PARCHMENT PAPER ON THE COUNTER. THE DOUGH WILL NOT STICK TO THE KITCHEN COUNTER, AND IF YOU ARE USING FLOUR, YOU CAN JUST THROW OUT PARCHMENT PAPER WHEN YOU ARE DONW TO AVOID THE FLOUR MESS ON THE COUNTER.

Secret # 32

SHELL HARD-BOILED EGGS WITH EASE AND LESS MESS.

PLACE 1/4 CUP WATER AND A COOLED HARD-BOILED EGG IN A MASON JAR. CLOSE THE LID AND LIGHTLY SHAKE. THE SHELLS SHOULD COME OFF WITH EASE. POUR THE SHELLS AND WATER IN THE SINK FOR EASY CLEANUP.

SAVE MONEY

LIMITING WASTE AND COOKING ON A BUDGET
HAS NEVER BEEN EASIER

Secret # 33

SAVE YOUR STALE BREAD.

SAVE MONEY

IF BREAD GOES STALE, DON'T THROW IT OUT! RUN THE BREAD UNDER WATER UNTIL IT IS SOAKED THROUGH. WRAP THE BREAD IN TINFOIL AND BAKE AT 350 DEGREES OVEN FOR 15 MINUTES. THE BREAD WILL BE FLUFFY AND TASTE.

Secret # 34

DON'T WASTE AVOCADOS.

YOU CAN FREEZE AVOCADOS WHOLE OR IN CHUNKS. THEY WILL STAY GOOD FOR UP TO 6 MONTHS IN THE FREEZER. DEFROST THEM IN THE REFRIGERATOR AND ENJOY.

Secret #35

VEGGIE SCRAPS MAKE AMAZING VEGETABLE BROTH.

SAVE THE TOPS AND PEELS OF YOUR VEGGIES IN A ZIPLOCK BAG IN THE FREEZER. WHEN THE BAG IS FULL, PLACE THE SCRAPS IN A SLOW COOKER AND COVER WITH WATER. ADD 2 TEASPOONS EACH OF SALT AND PEPPER AND COOK ON LOW FOR 10 HOURS. THIS HELPS YOU SAVE MONEY ON CANNED OR PACKAGED BROTH AND HELPS CUT DOWN ON WASTE BY USING THE ENTIRE VEGETABLE. (FROZEN BROTH WILL STAY GOOD FOR UP TO 6 MONTHS.)

Secret # 36

MAKE YOUR OWN SUN-DRIED TOMATOES.

SAVE MONEY

TAKE 1 PINT OF CHERRY TOMATOES AND CUT EACH
TOMATO IN HALF. ADD 2 TABLESPOONS OLIVE OIL AND 1
TEASPOON EACH OF SALT, PEPPER, GARLIC POWDER, AND
OREGANO. MIX AND PLACE THE TOMATOES CUT-SIDE UP
ON A SHEET PAN. BAKE FOR 2 HOURS AT 250 DEGREES.
STORE IN THE REFRIGERATOR FOR UP TO 1 WEEK OR
FREEZE FOR UP TO 6 MONTHS.

Secret # 37

REVIVE LEFTOVER TORTILLAS.

SAVE MONEY

DO YOU HAVE LEFTOVER TORTILLAS? MICROWAVE A TORTILLA FOR 30 SECONDS IN A MICROWAVE-SAFE GLASS CUP OR MUG TO FORM A CRISPY TACO SHELL. USE EITHER FLOUR OR CORN TORTILLAS.

Secret # 38

GRATE YOUR OWN PARMESAN.

SAVE MONEY

BUY PARMESAN WHOLE, NOT GRATED. YOU CAN GRATE WHAT YOU NEED AND THEN WRAP THE REST IN PARCHMENT PAPER, PLACE IT IN AN AIR-TIGHT CONTAINER, AND FREEZE IT FOR UP TO 6 MONTHS. NO NEED TO THAW IT; YOU CAN GRATE THE FROZEN CHEESE DIRECTLY FROM THE FREEZER.

Secret # 39

SAVE YOUR PARMESAN RIND.

YOU CAN PUT YOUR PARMESAN RIND IN A ZIPLOCK BAG AND FREEZE IT. WHEN MAKING SOUP, PUT THE RIND IN WHILE THE SOUP IS SIMMERING; IT WILL MELT INTO THE LIQUID AND CREATE AN AMAZING UMAMI BROTH.

GET MORE JUICE OUT OF
YOUR LEMONS AND LIMES!

SAVE MONEY

PLACE LEMONS AND LIMES IN THE MICROWAVE FOR 30 SECONDS. THIS WILL MAKE THE MEMBRANES SOFTER AND PRODUCE MORE JUICE FOR YOUR RECIPES.

Secret #41

AVOID FREEZER-BURNED ICE CREAM.

AFTER OPENING YOUR TUB OF ICE CREAM, PLACE A ZIPLOCK BAG OVER IT BEFORE STORING IT IN THE FREEZER. THIS PREVENTS FREEZER BURN BECAUSE IT CREATES AN EXTRA BARRIER TO AVOID AIR GETTING INTO THE ICE CREAM.

Secret #42

SKIP THE PARCHMENT PAPER.

INSTEAD OF USING PARCHMENT PAPER, YOU CAN JUST USE A PAPER TOWEL WHEN BAKING WITH A SPRINGFORM OR CAKE PAN. (NOTE: THIS DOES NOT WORK FOR SHEET PAN DINNERS.) CUT THE PAPER TOWEL TO THE SIZE OF THE SPRINGFORM OR CAKE PAN, WET IT SLIGHTLY, AND LINE THE BOTTOM OF THE PAN WITH IT.

Secret #43

DON'T BUY MICROWAVE POPCORN.

BUY A BAG OF KERNELS! YOU WILL GET SO MUCH MORE POPCORN FOR LESS MONEY. YOU PAY APPROXIMATELY FOUR TIMES MORE FOR MICROWAVE POPCORN VERSUS KERNELS YOU CAN POP YOUR OWN.

Secret #44

FREEZE YOUR LEFTOVER GINGER.

DON'T THROW OUT UNUSED GINGER. YOU CAN FREEZE IT FOR UP TO 1 YEAR AND GRATE THE FROZEN GINGER ANYTIME YOU NEED IT.

Secret #45

FISH AND CHICKEN ARE CHEAPER WHEN YOU BUY THEM WHOLE.

SAVE MONEY

BUY WHOLE FISH AND CHICKEN. (YOU CAN USUALLY HAVE THE FISHMONGER DEBONE THE FISH OR THE BUTCHER BREAK DOWN THE CHICKEN FOR FREE!) FREEZE WHAT YOU DO NOT USE.

Secret #46

DON'T BUY A RICER.

TO MAKE MASHED POTATOES FLUFFIER, YOU CAN GRATE
THE POTATOES WITH A CHEESE GRATER INSTEAD OF
BUYING A RICER.

Secret #47

MAKE MORE GUACAMOLE FOR LESS MONEY.

USE HALF THE AMOUNT OF AVOCADOS IN YOUR RECIPE AND ADD 1 CAN OF WHITE BEANS, LIKE GARBANZO BEANS OR NORTHERN BEANS. THEN MASH AWAY. IT DOES NOT CHANGE THE FLAVOR AT ALL!

Secret #48

KEEP YOUR TOMATOES
FRESH FOR LONGER.

SAVE MONEY

PLACE TAPE OVER THE SPOT WHERE THE TOMATO'S STEM USED TO BE. THIS PREVENTS MOISTURE FROM GETTING IN AND HELPS THE TOMATO STAY FRESH LONGER.

Secret #49

SKIP THE LINERS.

NO NEED TO SPEND MONEY ON MUFFIN OR CUPCAKE LINERS. JUST USE PARCHMENT PAPER. CUT CIRCLES FROM THE PARCHMENT PAPER TO FIT THE MUFFIN TIN AND BAKE AWAY.

MAKE YOUR OWN CAKE FLOUR.

INSTEAD OF PURCHASING CAKE FLOUR, YOU CAN MAKE IT YOURSELF IF YOU HAVE FLOUR AND CORNSTARCH AT HOME. MEASURE 1 CUP FLOUR AND REMOVE 2 TABLESPOONS. ADD 2 TABLESPOONS CORNSTARCH AND MIX. THIS WILL SAVE YOU A TRIP TO THE STORE AND IT WILL BE LESS EXPENSIVE THAN BUYING CAKE FLOUR.

Secret #51

FROTH YOUR OWN MILK.

SAVE MONEY

INSTEAD OF BUYING A FANCY MILK FROTHER, ADD YOUR MILK OR CREAM TO A BLENDER AND BLEND ON HIGH FOR 1 MINUTE. ALTERNATIVELY, YOU CAN SHAKE THE MILK IN A MASON JAR UNTIL FROTHY (APPROXIMATELY 3-5 MINUTES).

Secret #52

DRY YOUR OWN HERBS.

SAVE MONEY

WHEN YOU HAVE LEFTOVER FRESH HERBS, DON'T THROW THEM OUT. CUT THEM AND PLACE THEM BETWEEN TWO DAMP PAPER TOWELS ON A MICROWAVE-SAFE PLATE. COOK FOR 30 SECONDS AND CHECK IF HERBS ARE DRY. IF NOT, CONTINUE TO COOK IN 10-SECOND INCREMENTS UNTIL DRY. THIS SHOULD TAKE NO MORE THAN 1 MINUTE. WHEN THEY ARE DONE, THE HERBS CAN BE STORED IN A JAR IN THE CABINET FOR UP TO 6 MONTHS.

Secret #53

RESCUE YOUR CRYSTALLIZED HONEY.

SAVE MONEY

IF YOUR JAR OF HONEY IS CRYSTALLIZED, DON'T THROW IT OUT. INSTEAD, PLACE THE JAR IN A POT OF SIMMERING WATER AND THE CRYSTALS SHOULD MELT. THIS SHOULD ONLY TAKE 5-10 MINUTES.

Secret #54

REVIVE YOUR OLD SPICES.

IF YOUR DRIED SPICES ARE PAST THE EXPIRATION DATE, TOAST THEM IN A DRY PAN FOR A COUPLE MINUTES ON MEDIUM HEAT, STIRRING OCCASIONALLY, TO BRING BACK THEIR FLAVOR.

Secret #55

SAVE YOUR VEGGIE SCRAPS.

WHEN YOU PEEL ROOT VEGGIES LIKE POTATOES AND CARROTS, DO NOT THROW OUT THE SCRAPS. PLACE THEM IN A BOWL AND MIX THEM WITH 2 TABLESPOONS OLIVE OIL AND 2 TEASPOONS EACH OF SALT AND GARLIC POWDER. LAY THEM OUT ON A SHEET PAN. BAKE FOR 10 MINUTES AT 425 DEGREES, MIX, AND BAKE FOR 10 MORE MINUTES. NOW YOU HAVE A CRISPY SNACK!

Secret #56

VINEGAR ALTERNATIVES.

DON'T THROW OUT YOUR PICKLE OR OLIVE JUICE! YOU CAN USE THEM IN PLACE OF VINEGAR WHEN MAKING DRESSINGS.

Secret #57

FREEZE YOUR BREAD CRUMBS.

MAKE YOUR BREAD CRUMBS LAST LONGER BY STORING THEM IN THE FREEZER! YOU CAN USE ADD THEM RIGHT FROM THE FREEZER IN YOUR RECIPES.

BUY FROZEN SHRIMP INSTEAD OF FRESH.

IT IS CHEAPER TO BUY FROZEN SHRIMP INSTEAD OF FRESH SHRIMP. MOST SHRIMP YOU BUY IN THE STORE ARE PREVIOUSLY FROZEN ANYWAY.

SAVE MONEY

Secret #59

WRAP YOUR CHEESE CORRECTLY.

SAVE MONEY

NEVER WRAP CHEESE TIGHTLY IN PLASTIC WRAP BECAUSE IT WILL TRAP MOISTURE ON THE CHEESE, CAUSING IT TO GO BAD MORE QUICKLY. WRAP IT IN WAX PAPER OR PARCHMENT PAPER AND IT WILL LAST LONGER IN THE REFRIGERATOR.

Secret #60

KEEP YOUR COOKIES AND CAKE FRESH LONGER.

STORE COOKIES, CAKES, AND OTHER BAKED GOODS WITH A SLICE OF BREAD. THE BREAD WILL ABSORB THE MOISTURE, HELPING YOUR BAKED GOODS STAY FRESH LONGER.

Secret #61

ADD MARSHMALLOWS TO YOUR BROWN SUGAR.

TO PREVENT YOUR BROWN SUGAR FROM HARDENING, JUST ADD 3 BIG MARSHMALLOWS IN THE BAG BEFORE STORING.

BEEF UP YOUR BEEF.

TO STRETCH YOUR GROUND BEEF AND OTHER GROUND MEATS, ADD MUSHROOMS TO A FOOD PROCESSOR AND PULSE. COOK THE MUSHROOMS WITH THE GROUND BEEF, GROUND CHICKEN, OR GROUND TURKEY FOR TACOS, MEATLOAF, AND OTHER DISHES. THIS MAKES MORE FOOD AND STRETCHES THE DINNER FOR MORE MEALS.

Secret #63

MAKE AN "EAT NOW" BASKET.

KEEP AN "EAT NOW" BASKET IN YOUR REFRIGERATOR FOR
FOOD THAT HAS A SHORTER SHELF LIFE SO YOU DO NOT
WASTE FOOD YOU PAID FOR.

Secret #64

MAKE YOUR OWN SPICE MIXES.

YOU CAN MAKE YOUR OWN SPICE MIXES, LIKE TACO
SEASONING, STEAK SEASONING, ETC. YOU PROBABLY HAVE
THE SPICES IN THE PANTRY, AND THERE ARE A LOT OF
SIMPLE RECIPES ONLINE.

Secret #65

TOMATO PASTE TUBE HACK.

USE A ROLLING PIN TO SQUEEZE OUT THE TUBE OF
TOMATO PASTE WHEN IT GETS TOWARD THE END
OF THE TUBE. YOU WILL GET A COUPLE OF EXTRA
SERVINGS THIS WAY.

Secret #66

STORE APPLES AND POTATOES TOGETHER.

APPLES EXUDE A GAS CALLED ETHYLENE, SO STORING THEM TOGETHER PREVENTS POTATOES FROM SPROUTING, MAKING THEM LAST LONGER.

SAVE TIME

QUICK AND EASY IS THE NAME OF THE GAME

SAVE DISHES

SAVE MONEY

SAVE TIME

Secret #67

THICK SOUP WITHOUT THE ROUX.

IF YOU WANT TO THICKEN SOUP QUICKLY WITHOUT
HAVING TO MAKE A FLOUR SLURRY, JUST ADD 1/4 CUP
INSTANT POTATOES. THE SOUP WILL THICKEN IN 1 MINUTE.

SAVE TIME

Secret #68

MAKE LOTS OF BURGERS WITH LESS WORK.

MIX 3 POUNDS OF MEAT ON A SHEET PAN WITH YOUR FAVORITE BURGER SEASONINGS AND 2 TEASPOONS EACH OF SALT AND PEPPER. PRESS DOWN ON THE MEAT TO COVER THE ENTIRE SHEET PAN. BAKE AT 400 DEGREES FOR 10 MINUTES. ADD CHEESE AND BAKE FOR 2 MORE MINUTES. CUT INTO SQUARES TO EAT AS SLIDERS.

SAVE TIME

Secret #69

NO NEED TO BOIL RAVIOLI.

SAVE THE 20 MINUTES YOU USUALLY WAIT FOR THE WATER TO BOIL WHILE COOKING PASTA. JUST PUT FROZEN RAVIOLI IN THE SAUCE HEATING ON THE STOVE AND STIR. IN ABOUT 4 MINUTES, IT WILL COOK PERFECTLY. YOU'LL HAVE FEWER DISHES TO WASH AND YOU WILL SPEND LESS TIME COOKING.

SAVE TIME

Secret #70

SIX-MINUTE SALMON.

PLACE A SALMON FILET THAT IS 1 INCH TO 1 1/2 INCHES THICK SKIN-SIDE DOWN IN A COLD PAN WITH 2 TABLESPOONS OLIVE OIL AND 2 TABLESPOONS BUTTER. TURN THE STOVE TO MEDIUM HEAT; WHEN YOU START TO HEAR THE SALMON SIZZLE, START A TIMER FOR 3 MINUTES. WHEN THE TIMER RINGS, FLIP THE SALMON SKIN-SIDE UP AND COOK FOR ANOTHER 3 MINUTES.

SAVE TIME

Secret #71

CUT ONIONS FASTER WITHOUT CRYING.

BITE ONTO A SLICE OF BREAD WHILE CUTTING ONIONS. YOU CAN CUT UP AS MANY ONIONS AS YOU WANT WITHOUT THE TEARS AND WITHOUT HAVING TO STOP BECAUSE YOUR EYES ARE BURNING.

SAVE TIME

Secret #72

CORE ICEBERG LETTUCE EASILY.

TO CORE ICEBERG LETTUCE QUICKLY, SMASH IT STEM-SIDE DOWN ON THE KITCHEN COUNTER. THE CORE SHOULD SEPARATE EASILY. PULL THE CORE OUT AND ENJOY!

SAVE TIME

Secret #73

SEED A JALAPEÑO WITH EASE.

TO SEED A JALAPEÑO QUICKLY, ROLL THE JALAPEÑO WITH LIGHT PRESSURE ON THE COUNTER AND THEN TAP THE BOTTOM (THE STEM SIDE) TEN TIMES WITH A LITTLE FORCE. CUT FROM THE STEM SIDE OF THE JALAPEÑO AND THE SEEDS WILL POUR OUT.

NATURAL NUT BUTTER HACK.

TO ELIMINATE THE LIQUID THAT SITS ON TOP OF THE NUT BUTTER, LEAVE THE JAR UPSIDE DOWN. ALL THE LIQUID WILL COME TO THE BOTTOM OF THE JAR (NOW THE TOP), MAKING THE NUT BUTTER EASIER TO SPREAD.

SAVE TIME

Secret #75

TWO-INGREDIENT BREAD PUDDING.

CUT A SWEET BREAD (LEMON, CHOCOLATE, OR BABKA) LOAF INTO SMALL 1-INCH CHUNKS. MELT 16 OUNCES OF YOUR FAVORITE ICE CREAM AND MIX IT TOGETHER WITH THE BABKA IN A CASSEROLE DISH. LET IT SIT OVERNIGHT IN THE REFRIGERATOR THE DAY BEFORE YOU WANT TO EAT IT OR ON THE COUNTER FOR 1 HOUR THE SAME DAY. BAKE AT 350 DEGREES FOR 25 MINUTES AND ENJOY.

SAVE TIME

Secret #76

SET AND FORGET BIG BATCHES OF CARAMELIZED ONIONS.

INSTEAD OF MAKING CARAMELIZED ONIONS FOR ONE RECIPE, WHICH IS VERY TIME-CONSUMING, MAKE THEM IN BULK. IN A SLOW COOKER, PLACE 3 POUNDS OF SLICED ONIONS, 1 TABLESPOON THYME (CHOPPED), 2 CLOVES OF GARLIC (CRUSHED), 2 TABLESPOONS BROWN SUGAR, 2 TABLESPOONS BUTTER, 1 TEASPOON BALSAMIC VINEGAR, 1 TEASPOON SALT, AND 1 TEASPOON PEPPER. COVER AND COOK FOR 10 HOURS ON LOW. WHEN DONE, FREEZE IN BATCHES AND DEFROST WHEN NEEDED.

SAVE TIME

Secret #77

ONE-INGREDIENT WAFFLES.

NO NEED TO MIX UP A BATTER. TAKE COLD PUFF PASTRY AND CUT IT TO THE SIZE OF THE WAFFLE MAKER. PLACE IT IN THE WAFFLE MAKER FOR 5 MINUTES. IT WILL PUFF UP AND TASTE DELICIOUS.

SAVE TIME

Secret #78

DON'T BOIL THE GNOCCHI.

SAVE THE STEP OF BOILING YOUR GNOCCHI! JUST MIX FROZEN OR FRESH GNOCCHI ON A SHEET PAN WITH YOUR FAVORITE VEGGIES, 3 TABLESPOONS OF OLIVE OIL, AND YOUR FAVORITE SEASONINGS ON A SHEET PAN FOR A ONE-PAN MEAL. BAKE AT 400 DEGREES FOR 20 MINUTES, AND DINNER IS SERVED.

SAVE TIME

Secret #79

USE PESTO AS A BASE.

FOR A SIMPLE MULTIPURPOSE DRESSING OR MARINADE, JUST TAKE 4 TABLESPOONS PESTO AND MIX WITH 1/2 CUP EACH OF OLIVE OIL AND LEMON JUICE. PESTO ALREADY HAS ALL THE HERBS, GARLIC, AND CHEESE THAT YOU WILL NEED.

SAVE TIME

FROZEN RAVIOLI LASAGNA HACK.

INSTEAD OF BOILING LASAGNA NOODLES, USE FROZEN RAVIOLI AND LAYER THEM IN PLACE OF THE NOODLES. YOU DON'T EVEN NEED TO DEFROST OR BOIL THEM. THEY WILL COOK WITH THE REST OF THE LASAGNA.

SAVE TIME

Secret #81

NO-COOK MARINARA SAUCE.

PLACE 28 OUNCES CANNED WHOLE TOMATOES, 12 LEAVES FRESH BASIL, 1 TABLESPOON GARLIC POWDER, 1 TABLESPOON DRIED OREGANO, 1/2 TABLESPOON RED PEPPER FLAKES, 1 TEASPOON SALT, 1 TEASPOON PEPPER, AND 1 TABLESPOON OLIVE OIL IN A BOWL. SQUEEZE THE WHOLE TOMATOES WITH YOUR HANDS OR USE A POTATO MASHER. USE IT ON PIZZA OR ADD TO YOUR FAVORITE PASTA. YOU CAN ALSO FREEZE IT FOR UP TO 6 MONTHS SO YOU CAN USE IT IN OTHER RECIPES.

Secret #82

THE TRICK TO CUTTING RAW SQUASH.

TO MAKE CUTTING RAW SQUASH MUCH EASIER AND FASTER, USE A FORK TO POKE HOLES ALL OVER THE SQUASH. PLACE THE SQUASH IN THE MICROWAVE FOR 3 MINUTES. THIS SOFTENS THE SQUASH WITHOUT COOKING IT AND MAKES IT MUCH EASIER TO CUT.

SAVE TIME

Secret #83

STUFFED BREAD WITH NO KNEADING, STIRRING, OR WAITING FOR IT TO RISE.

TAKE PUFF PASTRY AND CUT IT INTO FOUR STRIPS. PLACE SCALLION CREAM CHEESE IN THE MIDDLE OF EACH STRIP AND THEN FOLD OVER THE EDGES TO SEAL. ROPE THE STRIPS AROUND EACH OTHER TO MAKE A BRAID. BRUSH THE DOUGH WITH EGG WASH AND SPRINKLE WITH EVERYTHING SEASONING. BAKE AT 400 DEGREES FOR 20 MINUTES.

SAVE TIME

Secret #84

FROZEN BEEF IS EASIER TO SLICE.

HERE IS A GREAT WAY TO MAKE SLICING RAW BEEF
SUPER EASY AND PRECISE: FREEZE YOUR BEEF FOR
20 MINUTES. WHEN YOU TAKE IT OUT TO SLICE, THE
MEAT WILL BE EASIER AND FASTER TO CUT.

SAVE TIME

Secret #85

FIFTEEN-MINUTE NO-BURN GARLIC BREAD.

CUT A BAGUETTE IN HALF. IN A BOWL, MIX 1 STICK SOFTENED BUTTER WITH 1 TABLESPOON GARLIC POWDER, AND 1 TEASPOON EACH OF OREGANO, SALT, AND PEPPER. SMEAR THE MIXTURE ON BOTH SLICES OF THE BAGUETTE. BAKE ON THE MIDDLE RACK FOR 15 MINUTES AT 350 DEGREES.

SAVE TIME

EIGHT-MINUTE SHEET PAN STEAK.

SET THE OVEN TO 500 DEGREES. SEASON STEAK WITH YOUR FAVORITE SEASONINGS PLUS 2 TEASPOONS EACH OF SALT AND PEPPER. DRIZZLE OLIVE OIL ALL OVER THE STEAK. BAKE ON THE TOP RACK FOR 4 MINUTES, FLIP, AND COOK FOR 4 MORE MINUTES FOR A PERFECT MEDIUM-RARE TEMPERATURE.

SAVE TIME

Secret #87

FASTER SHRIMP PARM.

ADD 1 1/2 POUNDS OF RAW SHRIMP TO A CASSEROLE DISH AND MIX IN 2 TABLESPOONS OLIVE OIL, 1 TEASPOON RED PEPPER FLAKES, 1/4 CUP GRATED PARMESAN, AND 2 TEASPOONS EACH OF GARLIC POWDER, SALT, PEPPER, AND OREGANO. MIX AND SPREAD OUT EVENLY ON A SHEET PAN. COVER SHRIMP WITH 2 CUPS OF YOUR FAVORITE MARINARA SAUCE AND TOP WITH 2 CUPS MOZZARELLA. BAKE AT 400 DEGREES FOR 15 MINUTES.

EASY STUFFED MUSHROOMS.

MIX BUTTON MUSHROOMS (STEMS REMOVED) WITH 2 TEASPOONS EACH OF SALT, PEPPER, AND GARLIC POWDER. PLACE THE MUSHROOMS ONTO A BAKING SHEET. ADD ABOUT 1 TEASPOON PICO DE GALLO TO EACH MUSHROOM AND BAKE AT 400 DEGREES FOR 20 MINUTES.

SAVE TIME

Secret #89

FLUFFIEST MASHED POTATO HACK.

WHEN MAKING MASHED POTATOES, ADD 1 TEASPOON
BAKING POWDER RIGHT BEFORE YOU MASH THEM. THIS
WILL MAKE YOUR MASHED POTATOES THE FLUFFIEST
THEY HAVE EVER BEEN.

SAVE TIME

Secret #90

JUICY MEATBALL HACK.

INSTEAD OF USING BREAD SOAKED IN MILK IN YOUR MEATBALL RECIPE, REPLACE IT WITH 1/2 CUP RICOTTA AND 1/2 CUP BREAD CRUMBS. THE CHEESE MELTS INTO THE MEAT AND KEEPS IT MOIST.

SAVE TIME

Secret #91

HULL STRAWBERRIES QUICKLY!

USE A PLASTIC OR METAL STRAW AND PUSH IT THROUGH THE STRAWBERRY FROM THE BOTTOM (THE POINTY SIDE) TO THE TOP (THE STEM SIDE). THE HULL AND THE STEM WILL COME OUT WITH EASE.

SAVE TIME

Secret #92

TASTIER TATERS WITHOUT THE EXTRA WORK.

WHEN MAKING MASHED OR CRISPY POTATOES, YOU CAN MAKE THEM MORE FLAVORFUL IF YOU BOIL THEM IN BROTH INSTEAD OF JUST WATER. PLUS, BOILING POTATOES FIRST MAKES THEM BAKE FASTER!

SAVE TIME

Secret #93

EASY S'MORE CHEESECAKE.

TAKE A STORE-BOUGHT CHEESECAKE. MELT 1 CUP
CHOCOLATE IN THE MICROWAVE AT 30-SECOND
INTERVALS UNTIL FULLY MELTED. POUR CHOCOLATE
OVER THE CHEESECAKE. SPRINKLE A HANDFUL
OF CRUMBLED GRAHAM CRACKERS ACROSS THE
TOP OF THE CAKE AND FINISH OFF THE TOP WITH
MARSHMALLOWS. PLACE ON THE TOP RACK IN THE
OVEN AT 450 DEGREES FOR 2 MINUTES TO CHAR THE
MARSHMALLOWS. ENJOY!

SAVE TIME

Secret #94

POACH YOUR EGGS IN BATCHES.

USE A MUFFIN TIN TO MAKE A BUNCH OF POACHED EGGS PERFECTLY AT ONCE. PUT 2 TABLESPOONS WATER IN EACH MUFFIN TIN SECTION AND CRACK AN EGG INTO EACH SECTION. BAKE FOR 13 MINUTES AT 350 DEGREES.

SAVE TIME

Secret #95

CRISPY CHICKEN HACK.

GET CRISPY OVEN-BAKED CHICKEN WINGS BY ADDING
1 TABLESPOON BAKING POWDER WHEN YOU ARE
SEASONING THE CHICKEN. THIS KEEPS THE SKIN DRY
SO IT CRISPS UP FASTER IN THE OVEN.

SAVE TIME

Secret #96

FIVE-INGREDIENT TACO RICE IN FIVE MINUTES.

FRY UP 1 POUND OF CHORIZO IN 1 TEASPOON OIL. ADD 2 CUPS COOKED RICE, 3 SCALLIONS (CHOPPED), AND THE JUICE OF 1 LIME. YOU CAN ADD SOME CILANTRO TOO. A DELICIOUS MEAL IN UNDER 5 MINUTES!

SAVE TIME

Secret #97

BOOZY RED WINE CHOCOLATE FONDUE.

IN A POT, MELT 3 TABLESPOONS BUTTER ON LOW HEAT. ADD 1/2 CUP OF YOUR FAVORITE RED WINE, 12 OUNCES SEMISWEET CHOCOLATE, 1 TEASPOON SALT, AND 2 TABLESPOONS ORANGE OR RASPBERRY JAM. MELT AND STIR FOR 3 MINUTES UNTIL THE CHOCOLATE IS FULLY MELTED. ENJOY WITH FUN THINGS TO DIP (PRETZELS, POUND CAKE, FRUIT, ETC.) FOR A SIMPLE AND FAST DESSERT.

SAVE TIME

Secret #98

HEALTHY AND DELICIOUS ICE CREAM IN A RUSH.

NO NEED TO WAIT FOR ICE CREAM TO CHURN! ADD 2 CUPS OF YOUR FAVORITE FROZEN FRUIT AND 2 FROZEN BANANAS TO A BLENDER AND BLEND UNTIL CREAMY. GENTLY MIX IN 1/2 CUP CHOCOLATE CHIPS AND ENJOY.

SAVE TIME

Secret #99

APPLE CORER FRY HACK.

USE YOUR APPLE CORER TO CUT FRIES QUICKLY AND
EVENLY. PLUS, THEY WILL COOK MORE UNIFORMLY
WHEN THEY ARE EVENLY SLICED.

Secret #100

QUICK AND EASY RISOTTO.

CUT 20 MINUTES OFF THE TIME IT TAKES TO MAKE RISOTTO! USE YOUR FAVORITE RISOTTO RECIPE BUT REPLACE THE RICE AND LIQUID WITH 2 CUPS ORZO AND 3 CUPS BROTH. ADD ALL THE BROTH AT ONCE (NO NEED TO HEAT IT UP FIRST) AND COOK THE MIXTURE ON MEDIUM-HIGH HEAT. WHEN IT COMES TO A LIGHT BOIL, COOK FOR 10 MINUTES AND STIR A COUPLE OF TIMES. ADD BUTTER, CHEESE, AND WHATEVER ELSE YOUR RECIPE CALLS FOR AND ENJOY!

SAVE TIME

GRILL YOUR PIZZA.

MAKE PIZZA FAST BY GRILLING IT. ROLL OUT PIZZA DOUGH AND BRUSH OIL ON BOTH SIDES. ADD IT TO A HOT GRILL AND COOK FOR 2 MINUTES. FLIP AND ADD MARINARA SAUCE (ABOUT 3 TABLESPOONS), A HANDFUL OF MOZZARELLA, AND YOUR FAVORITE TOPPINGS. CLOSE THE GRILL AND COOK FOR 2 MORE MINUTES.

SAVE TIME

Bon appétit !

OTHER KITCHEN HACKS TO REMEMBER:

_____

_____

_____

_____

_____

_____

_____

_____

_____

JASON GOLDSTEIN IS A CHIROPRACTOR BY DAY AND FOOD BLOGGER BY NIGHT.

THROUGH HIS CULINARY BLOG, *CHOP HAPPY*, JASON SHARES HIS LOVE OF EASY COMFORT FOOD RECIPES, SHOWCASING RICH FLAVORS, INVENTIVE IDEAS, AND UNIQUE COOKING TIPS AND ADVICE. HE WAS A FINALIST ON SEASON 14 OF *FOOD NETWORK STAR* AND FINISHED IN THE TOP 10 IN RACHAEL RAY'S COOKBOOK CONTEST. HIS RECIPES HAVE BEEN FEATURED ON *THE CHEW* AND *THE KITCHEN*, AND HE HAS APPEARED ON *GOOD MORNING AMERICA*. LIVING IN NEW YORK CITY AND THE HAMPTONS, JASON ENJOYS TESTING RECIPES ON HIS HUSBAND, TOM, AND GRABBING FRENCH FRIES BY THE HANDFUL.

ABOUT FAMILIUS

VISIT OUR WEBSITE: WWW.FAMILIUS.COM

FAMILIUS IS A GLOBAL TRADE PUBLISHING COMPANY THAT PUBLISHES BOOKS AND OTHER CONTENT TO HELP FAMILIES BE HAPPY. WE BELIEVE THAT HAPPY FAMILIES ARE KEY TO A BETTER SOCIETY AND THE FOUNDATION OF A HAPPY LIFE. WE RECOGNIZE THAT EVERY FAMILY LOOKS DIFFERENT AND PASSIONATELY BELIEVE IN HELPING ALL FAMILIES FIND GREATER JOY, WHATEVER THEIR SITUATION. TO THAT END, WE PUBLISH BEAUTIFUL BOOKS THAT HELP FAMILIES LIVE OUR 10 HABITS OF HAPPY FAMILY LIFE: *LOVE TOGETHER, PLAY TOGETHER, LEARN TOGETHER, WORK TOGETHER, TALK TOGETHER, HEAL TOGETHER, READ TOGETHER, EAT TOGETHER, GIVE TOGETHER,* AND *LAUGH TOGETHER.* FURTHER, FAMILIUS DOES NOT DISCRIMINATE ON THE BASIS OF RACE, COLOR, RELIGION, GENDER, AGE, NATIONALITY, DISABILITY, CASTE, OR SEXUAL ORIENTATION IN ANY OF ITS ACTIVITIES OR OPERATIONS. FOUNDED IN 2012, FAMILIUS IS LOCATED IN SANGER, CALIFORNIA.

CONNECT

FACEBOOK: WWW.FACEBOOK.COM/FAMILIUSBOOKS
PINTEREST: WWW.PINTEREST.COM/FAMILIUSBOOKS
INSTAGRAM: @FAMILIUSBOOKS
TIKTOK: @FAMILIUSBOOKS

FAMILIUS

"THE MOST IMPORTANT WORK YOU EVER DO WILL BE WITHIN THE WALLS OF YOUR OWN HOME."